A STRAIGHTFORWARD GUIDE
TO

THE TWO MINUTE MESSAGE

EFFECTIVE PRESENTATIONS UNDER PRESSURE

WILLIAM FREEMAN

STRAIGHTFORWARD PUBLISHING
www.straightforwardco.uk

Straightforward Publishing
38 Cromwell Road
London E17 9JN

© William Freeman 2001
Reprinted 2001

All rights reserved. No part of this publication may be reproduced in a retrieval system, or transmitted by any means, electronic or mechanical, photocopying or otherwise, without the prior permission of the copyright holder.

British Library Cataloguing in Publication Data. A catalogue record of this book is available from the British library.

ISBN 1899924 73 6

Printed by Polestar Scientifica Exeter

Cover design by Straightforward Graphics

Cartoons by Waldorf
www.cartoonists.co.uk/waldorf

Whilst every effort has been taken to ensure that information in this book was correct at the time of going to press, the author and publishers accept no responsibility for errors or omissions contained within.

THE TWO-MINUTE MESSAGE
By
William Freeman

PREFACE

There are many challenges associated with putting across a convincing sales story and there are many very good books describing the skills and techniques needed to do so.

This book focuses on one important aspect of the selling process. It describes an easy technique to get your customer interested in what you have to say; the first essential step in any sales process. It then shows how you can use this technique to make your point effectively.

There's no 'rocket science' in this book. Nor are there academic theories that look fine on paper but are difficult to apply in the real world. The Two-Minute Message technique is based on years of practice and observation, plus a fair amount of experience and scar tissue. It makes sense and it works. Guaranteed.

How many times have you experienced the dubious thrill of people trying to sell to you when you haven't the slightest interest in what they have to offer? There seems to be some strange law that works on the principle of the lower the client interest, the longer the sales story. That's how it seems to me anyway.

Whatever you are 'selling', you must be able to crystallise your sales message into an effective synopsis that will arouse your customer's interest in what you have to say. We have called this synopsis the 'two minute message' (TMM for short), and this book will tell you how and where to apply it.

This subject is relevant to anyone with a product to sell, a case to put over, or just an interesting story to tell. The TMM process won't win you sales by itself, but it will help you create the situation where your sales story can be heard. Arousing interest, of course, is valueless unless you follow it with a persuasive and compelling message and the TMM process will help you there too.

Businesses are popping up all over the place these days. Sadly, some are also falling by the wayside. Existing businesses, large and small, are repositioning themselves in the marketplace and striving to show how they differ from their competition. The TMM principle applies to these situations too. Every business needs a brief and compelling message that positions its purpose and value. So my TMM process isn't just for direct sales people; it is relevant to every business person operating in a competitive environment.

Lots of people have contributed to this book, directly or indirectly. I would like to thank my business partners, my colleagues and all my past and present clients, many of whom have suffered at the receiving end of my verbal excesses, insensitive intrusions and general ranting. My experiences with these people verified the need for the two-minute message technique.

I would like to thank too, all the students that I have worked with, trying to teach how the TMM process can be applied in the real world. As always, I learned far more from these people than they did from me.

My thanks too go to 'Waldorf' for providing the cartoon illustrations for this book - a talented young man with a great future. You can see more of his cartoon work at www.cartoonists.co.uk/waldorf

All of the anecdotes and stories that I use in this book are based on genuine experiences so I cannot make the standard disclaimer that every character is fictitious and bears no resemblance to any person living or dead. Faces and memories were flashing through my mind as I was writing this book.

All of my 'fictitious-but-based-on-reality' characters come out of it pretty well though - apart from me that is. I wish that I had discovered the two minute message technique many years ago.

I hope that you enjoy the book and that you benefit from it. Any comments that you have would be most welcome, so please feel free to contact me. Tell me your success stories and I'll include them in the next reprint.

Good luck.

William Freeman
Hampton
Middlesex
UK

Email wdf@cambridge-associates.co.uk
www.cambridge-associates.co.uk
www.TwoMinuteMessage.com

THE TWO MINUTE MESSAGE

TABLE OF CONTENTS

1. Today's Business Environment — **9**
   - A fast moving world — 9
   - Demands on our time — 11
   - Why we need more than a 'good story' — 13
   - Case 1 'the supplier selection challenge' — 16
   - Case 2 'the nervous managing director' — 19
   - The need to establish value — 20
   - Social calls and business calls — 20
   - How to use this book — 23

2. The Tale of Tommy — **27**
   - What this section is all about — 27
   - Tommy gets ready — 27
   - The 'introductory summary' situation — 28
   - The 'elevator challenge' — 33
   - The 'set piece' story — 38
   - The presentation creation problem — 43
   - The lessons for Tommy — 47

3. The Two Minute Message concept — **49**
   - Using a TMM to arouse interest — 50
   - The TMM as a set piece message — 51
   - The TMM as a promotional letter — 54
   - Using the TMM to plan a major presentation or event — 56

4. Building Your TMM (the TMM recipe book) — **59**
   - The OATS principle — 59
   - Defining your 'SMART' objective — 59
   - The 'DRACHMA' definition of a good objective — 62
   - TMM objective vs. campaign objective — 62

-	The 'Four M' definition of resources	64
-	Your target audience	65
-	External and internal candidates	65
-	Analysing your audience	66
-	The Themes of your Message	67
-	Themes versus 'Facts'	68
-	'Strengths' & 'Uniques'	69
-	Tests for selection	72
-	The TMM Building Blocks	73
-	The TMM four part structure	74
-	Your audience context statement	74
-	Examples of audience context statement	75
-	Your Key Theme	77
-	Why only a single theme?	78
-	Your Supporting Themes	79
-	Your Closing Statement	80

5. Identifying your TMM topics — **83**
- Your three strands of possible value — 84
- Topic examples — 85
- My list of TMM topics (worksheet) — 87

6. Pulling it all together (the busy person's summary guide) — **89**
- Definition of a two minute message — 89
- When you would use it — 89
- The OATS sequence — 90
- The four part structure for a TMM — 92
- Taking things forward — 92

7. APPENDIX — **94**
- Blank TMM proforma
- Case examples
- Overview of Cambridge Associates

1
TODAY'S BUSINESS ENVIRONMENT

A FAST MOVING WORLD

There is an incredibly frantic nature to business these days, or so it seems to me. People seem to be dashing about all over the place, responding to the beck and call of their mobile phones, electronic pagers, palmtop computers, bleeping tie-pins and all the other wonderful gee-whiz technologies that we have today.

Come to think of it, these business people aren't just dashing about while they are doing all this furious communicating. They do it in restaurants, on trains, whilst walking the dog and when they are lying on the beach. Some people even do it when they are sitting on the lavatory. Or so I'm told!

No doubt these very busy people are responding to somebody else's demand for instant attention, and during any quieter moments that they have, they will use these same technologies to make similar demands on other people.

There was a time (long ago) when driving your car or travelling by train meant that you could not be contacted. In my early days working for IBM we had 'central message boards' and I got into the routine of picking up my messages twice a day, possibly even three times when things were very busy. Secretaries would answer the telephone and say things like, 'I'm sorry he's gone for the day, can I take a message for him to collect tomorrow morning?'

It worked OK in those days; our clients understood the situation and they accepted it. They worked on the same principles themselves. These 'old fashioned' communication methods weren't perfect of course. One time when I was away on a two week holiday, a new young lady working on the message desk informed one of my clients that I was in the lavatory and that I would call her back in a few moments. When I saw my client next, she seemed rather concerned about my state of health. I guess that's understandable if she thought I had spent the last ten days or so performing some amazing (and ongoing) bodily function. My client had forgotten why she called me in the first place but that didn't seem to matter. Customers didn't demand 'real time' attention in those days - unless they had an urgent problem of course.

Life is very different today. Technology has given us the means to communicate as and when we want to but, in this new pace of business life, we are in danger of losing some of the disciplines of patience and restraint.

If we are to believe what we read, business life in the twenty first century is likely to become more frantic. Pundits say that this kind of technology will be even more widely available in the future; we can expect it to be built into our clothing, incorporated in our wrist watches, blended into our teeth fillings and imprinted on the back of our contact lenses. If you are wearing it, it is likely to be WAP enabled. As the old saying goes, 'we ain't seen nothing yet!' Sounds fun, doesn't it?

This isn't a Luddite rant against technology by the way; I am a great fan. After all, a major part of my consultancy business depends on it. I am convinced that all of these developments will add enormous value to our business and personal lives, giving us the freedom to communicate as and when we want to.

Of course, it isn't just technology that is affecting how we live and work. Modern businesses are constantly reinventing themselves. In this competitive age, to stand still is to die. 'If it ain't broke, don't fix it' isn't a valid philosophy anymore. 'Break it regularly and rebuild it differently' is a more valid view.

A few years ago, who would have thought that we would be able to bank our money with the local supermarket, order anything we need via a home computer, pay our bills in the middle of the night and get our gas services from the local electricity company.

A business client told me recently that more than half of his current revenue is coming from products and services that didn't exist two years ago.

It's a changing world and it's a busy world.

DEMANDS ON OUR TIME

As a consequence of all these changes, the demands on our time are increasing dramatically. The volume of information that hits us at home and at work is growing day by day. And it isn't all high quality information that we are getting - far from it. Unless we take positive steps to prevent it, we find ourselves at the receiving end of junk mail, junk faxes, junk email and unsolicited telephone calls offering all sorts of products and services that we thought we could live without.

Nowadays we have to protect our time carefully to keep out all of these unwanted intrusions. We haven't the time, energy or inclination to give them all our full attention. And it's exactly the same situation for our clients. Most business people have full diaries and a demand for even more appointments and meetings. Those with savvy keep their diaries under strict control and value the time they have for themselves.

As sales people, we should expect to have to work hard to get time with our clients and we must be able to justify the time that we take.

If you are in a job or profession where you sell your time (doctors and lawyers for example), then perhaps you can operate an 'open-diary' system. You start the year with a big blank book, each day is divided into fifteen minute slots and away you go. You are open for business and it's first come, first served. If the demand is high you can raise your price and if you are worth it, people will pay.

I wonder how sales people would react if their clients put a value on their time and charged accordingly. Not a bad idea. Perhaps I should tell my clients who have cash flow problems to try it out!

Professional business people don't work on an open diary system. They keep diaries for their own benefit. They use them to plan how they will allocate their own time to achieve their objectives. They employ

TODAY'S BUSINESS ENVIRONMENT

secretaries, personal assistants and other 'gatekeepers' to help them manage and protect this valuable time - especially from enthusiastic sales people. All good sales training courses will tell you to spend time with these 'gatekeepers' and to cultivate them. You don't mind if your competitors are turned away, as long as you are allowed to meet the senior decision-makers. But earning that right isn't easy.

Salesmen of bygone days will occasionally tell tales of how they could drift into a customer's office whenever they wanted to, and after a long and leisurely chat (and possibly a spot of lunch and a glass or two of wine) come away with a signed contract.

It probably wasn't ever quite that easy. Maybe I am suffering from selective memory but that's how I remember those halcyon days.

'Successful selling is all to do with having a good relationship', these veteran salesmen would say, 'if that is in good shape, you will have no trouble getting a slot in the customer's diary.'

There is undoubtedly some truth in that statement, but it is only part of the story.

WHY WE NEED MORE THAN A 'GOOD STORY'

It isn't good enough these days just having a good story to tell. Of course, as salespeople, it is crucial that we _can_ tell a good story, but it counts for nothing if we can't get an appropriate audience to want to listen to it. One thing for certain is that few people have the time (or indeed the inclination) to listen to every sales argument or to read a detailed report - no matter how good these might be.

These days there seem to be more business presentations than ever before: presentations to sell products, presentations to agree a strategy, presentations to review a situation and presentations to show a set of financial results. I'm not quite sure why that is so. Maybe we like to share information more than we used to. Or maybe the technology makes it easy to show lots of detailed information.

Whatever the reason, there are lots of business presentations.

In my experience, most of these events tend to be fairly dull and usually take far too long. Gone are the days when a business-person would regard a formal presentation as an enjoyable event, a break from the hassle and humdrum of day to day business life.

"What I used to like about being a senior executive," a established C.E.O. once told me, "was the time that I had to myself. I had lots of time to think and to reflect which, in many ways, is what my job is all about. I had the time to do what I was being paid for."

He went on to bemoan all the unnecessary intrusions that creep into current day to day executive life, and how he fought against them.

In one sense all sales people are intruders. They interrupt the processes of running a business. Of course, the good ones will add genuine value; the time that they take is more than justified by the value that they give in return.

But getting that time is a challenge. In business, we find ourselves competing for the time and for the attention of those people whom we wish to influence - especially that of our customers. And I am not just referring to 'customers' in a conventional sense (i.e. those folks that are kind enough to buy things from us from time to time).

There are many other 'internal customers' who are key to our success - departments in our organisation, team colleagues, business partners, outside suppliers and so on. We need to persuade these people to work with us and, in some situations, to help us by giving some of their resources.

TODAY'S BUSINESS ENVIRONMENT

The real winners in the competitive world of business are those people who can capture the imagination of their intended audience very quickly, thereby earning them the extra time that they need to present their complete story in all its grandeur. These people are able to summarise their points in such a compelling manner that their customer can hardly bear to wait to hear the rest of their story. OK, OK, that's probably a slight exaggeration so let's settle for the situation where the customer is willing to continue the discussion. We refer to this short, compelling summary as a 'two minute message'.

Brevity is important here too. The more we add to our sales story, the more we are in danger of diluting its impact. Sure, we need a full proposition that will explain all the benefits of our products and services but it isn't the detail or volume of words that make a message compelling. The detail might *justify* the story but it won't attract people to it in the first place. Or make it memorable.

'Less is More' is phrase that my art teacher used a lot. He wanted his students to use the minimum amount of paint and the fewest number of brush strokes to create the desired impression. A great message for the amateur painter. Most of us added too much colour and detail, thinking that every extra splash of colour would improve the final painting. It never did. In some cases, the blank canvas gave a better impression than the 'final' painting.

Adding too much detail can get you into a situation where the outcome is worse than if you had said nothing at all. I know, I've been there. Done it. Got the 'T' shirt and so on. So brevity is the key.

The Lord's Prayer has had a great impact on Western Society, yet it is only sixty-six words long. The European Commission report into market forces affecting the price of cabbages is over sixty-six thousand words. Now, there might be lots of valid detail in this document (oh yeah?) but its length doesn't make it one thousand times more memorable than the

Lord's Prayer. So if we want our message to have an impact, it needs to be brief and to the point.

This book will show you how to build an appealing synopsis for every critical business message that you have, giving you the wherewithal to engage the hearts and minds of those people that you want to impress.

That's only half the story of course. Once you've made a good impact and earned the extra time to tell your story in more detail, you mustn't waste it or abuse it. You must tell your more detailed tale in a compelling and persuasive manner, and give value for every minute that you take.

The TMM process will help you here too.

The following two case examples were the catalysts that started me thinking about this whole process.

CASE 1 - THE SUPPLIER SELECTION CHALLENGE

Some time ago I did a consultancy assignment for the sales manager of a large organisation. He wanted an information system to help him manage his sales force and, as you would expect, many prospective suppliers were beating at his door to try to sell him their respective products and services. My job was to whittle down these potential suppliers of undoubtedly wonderful solutions to a shortlist of two or three worthy candidates. This was good standard consultancy work from my point of view, but I suspect that my role was an irritant as far as the competing sales people were concerned. They wanted to deal with my client directly and not via an intermediary body. They would claim that working via me could dilute their story and that I wouldn't be able to show the true value that they could offer. Frankly, I don't blame them for having this opinion.

So what was the value of my role?

TODAY'S BUSINESS ENVIRONMENT

Graham, my client's sales manager, described his situation quite simply. "When I resist all these sales people and tell them that I am too busy to see them," he said, "they seem to think that I don't believe what they can do - so they intensify their efforts to get me to see them."

That made good sense to me. Any supplier worth his salt isn't going to give up without a good fight.

"They then start to bombard me with literature, brochures, business cases and things they call 'value propositions'," Graham continued.

Not forgetting reference client visits, internal references and product demonstrations if they've got any sense, I thought. As a trained salesman, I could see the logic of what these people were doing; they wanted the chance to prove their capabilities.

"You're absolutely right," Graham said when I pointed this out to him, "but that isn't the issue. The fact is, I _do_ believe what they are saying, I assume that they _can_ do everything that they claim." I think I started to rub my eyes at this point.

"My problem," Graham went on, "is that I don't have time to let every credible supplier organisation tell its story. I have a business to run and I need to be selective about who I give time to. Every bunch of people that we take seriously means that we have to give up time to listen to their story. We need to check their references, and we need to verify that their proposed solution can really do for us what they claim it is doing for some of their other clients. And so on. All of those activities take up time that we could deploy elsewhere for our own profit. I don't know what the cost of all that time and lost business opportunity amounts to, but we're probably talking around a hundred thousand pounds per supplier."

I didn't feel this was the right moment to discuss my consultancy fee, but I could see the point Graham was making. Senior business people want solutions that will help them, but they can't spare the time to listen to sales stories from every possible provider. If we are honest we must acknowledge that there are very few (and I mean very, very few) business opportunities that could only be satisfied by one solution provider.

A friend of mine once compared this selection dilemma to buying a suit of clothes.

"When you've found something you like," he said, "you will probably buy it. If the suit fits you and if it's the right colour and the right price and so on, you are happy. It doesn't have to be the only possible suit in the world that would meet your requirements. There could be a hundred other racks in a hundred other shops with equally good offers but you don't look at all of them before you make your choice, do you?"

I thought that was a very good point. I also made a note to discuss this story with my wife.

Of course, most business organisations will have a purchasing department responsible for evaluating potential suppliers and their offerings, and I am not belittling the importance of that task. As ambitious sales people, however, we want to establish personal relationships with our customer's senior executives. We want to get close enough to these people so that they regard us as credible business advisors. We want to get ourselves into a consultancy role so that we can save our customers from the dilemma of choice.

That means we must engage their interest about what we are capable of and the value that we can add to their business operations- and we must do this before our competitors take the initiative.

After all, we don't want to be in a position like one of those ninety-nine other suits gathering dust on ninety-nine unvisited racks.

CASE 2 - THE NERVOUS MANAGING DIRECTOR

I once had a consultancy assignment as a mentor to the managing director of a software company. I acted in the role of personal confidante; someone he could talk to and share ideas with, who wasn't enmeshed in any of the company politics and general infighting. A sort of business 'agony aunt', I suppose.

One of my client's sales people had arranged for my MD friend to meet the chief executive of a manufacturing organisation that was seeking some process design software.

"Every time I am asked to do this kind of sales call," my MD client said, "I get extremely nervous." That comment rather surprised me as he struck me as a pretty confident sort of chap.

"My sales people are relying on me to make a good impression with this CEO that will have a positive knock-on effect on our sales revenues," he continued. "If I don't succeed in doing that and if one of our competitors gets in the door, we could be locked out of this customer for several years. That's the nature of our business."

In these circumstances, making a good impact becomes pretty critical.

Being ignored (rather like one of the unvisited suits) doesn't necessarily happen because we have an inferior product or service. More often than not, it means that we haven't been able to tell our story to the right person, at the right time.

And that's the consequence of us not making the right impact, or not having created the opportunity to do so.

THE NEED TO ESTABLISH VALUE

Every salesperson knows that the early stage of any sales encounter is crucial. You know that during the first few moments of any customer meeting you must `earn the right' to carry on. Your customer may let the meeting continue out of courtesy, but you want him (or her) to believe that there is genuine value in doing so.

For much of my sales career, business people stressed the importance of building relationships at all levels within the customer organisation. Phrases like 'relationship management', 'relationship value' and 'executive contact programmes' were all the rage. They still are.

But client meetings must go beyond the boundaries of normal social contact.

SOCIAL CALLS AND BUSINESS CALLS

At one time in my career, I was an IBM sales manager looking after a major UK retail organisation. I had a team of people working with me and we were proud of our close relationship with the customer's staff; we

TODAY'S BUSINESS ENVIRONMENT

socialised with them, we drank with them and we had all sorts of friendly sporting contests between our two organisations.

I was surprised, therefore, when the customer's IS Director took me to one side and advised me 'to be careful'. "You are in danger of blurring some of the relationship boundaries," she told me.

I guess I must have looked puzzled so she went on to give her view on the differences between social and business relationships.

"Social contact tends to be casual," she said, "there is no formal agenda and the conversation is relaxed, friendly and free flowing. On the other hand, business contacts need be more structured and there has to be a purpose that _both_ parties deem to be worth spending time on."

She was absolutely right and I could see what she was getting at. Too often we just popped in to 'say hello' without any other evident planned purpose. It was all very pleasant social stuff mind you, but it took up lots of time and probably contributed very little business value as far as the customer was concerned.

I think too, that she was warning us about the image of our competitors who were bending over backwards to give a good impression and to offer genuine value. And that is what business calls are all about. Not formality, pomposity or unnecessary structure, but making sure that _every_ meeting gives the customer some value.

I remember a role play call I once did on an IBM sales training course. I had set my objective to gain lots of useful information that I could subsequently turn into sales opportunities.

"What a great sales call," I told everyone during the debriefing session. I usually made comments like that to try to boost the tutor's rating of my performance. I then went on to tell everybody how, by my incredibly clever questioning, I had discovered one hell of a lot about the customer's organisation.

When my tutor asked me to describe the value that the *customer* had got from the meeting, I was a bit stumped. I hadn't considered that.

So establishing your credibility, your purpose and your potential value is vital when you are calling on someone for the first time. Actually, it is pretty important every time, and it is what differentiates a social call from a business call.

Of course, this doesn't mean that you shouldn't have a social chat or banter at all with a client. In fact, it is vital that you do, since mentioning their holiday, kids or whatever shows that you can relate to them as individuals. But these strands of conversation should be warm-ups (warms up?) or postscripts to a meeting or phone call, not the sole purpose of either of these events. This is the point that my retail customer executive was making to me all those years ago.

Some people say that when you meet senior customer executives, all you have to do is ask a few key questions and they will immediately share all their problems with you. That approach could work in theory I suppose, but only after you have established a very close relationship with the customer and proven that you can add value.

People don't unburden themselves to anyone that happens to ask a pertinent question. They might do so with a doctor or a priest, because they recognise each of those roles as having skills that can help them. If you are in pain and you see a person wearing a doctor's white coat and carrying a stethoscope, you will tell that person your problem. You will answer and question fully and with great enthusiasm (assuming your condition allows it). You won't hold back any information.

A sales role isn't perceived as having the same kind of status (not automatically). Nevertheless, senior business people tend to be open-minded and they are happy to share confidences with consultants and other confidants whom they trust.

Establishing your credibility and your value are the foundations for establishing trust. And those things can all start from a two-minute message.

HOW TO USE THIS BOOK

You can probably read this book from cover to cover in a single sitting. I recommend that approach; it will probably take you about an hour to read the rest of the book. Or at least skim through it. If you are standing in a bookstore and you have read this far, then you could try to brazen it out until you have finished. But I suggest you buy the book because I'm going to recommend that you read it a second, or even a third time.

Some people have told me that they enjoyed reading it whilst soaking in the bath at the end of a long day, with a favourite cocktail to hand. You

THE TWO MINUTE MESSAGE

could even read it during your journey to work - assuming that you are travelling by train of course.

The second time you read this book, have a pen in your hand and make notes on any thoughts and ideas that strike you as useful. Scribble in the margins and in any gaps in the page that you can see (ignore what you were told at school about not writing on books). Not many books come with an invitation to scribble all over them, but this is a workbook designed to help you. It isn't a trophy book to display on your bookshelf or on your coffee table.

Besides, this isn't an expensive book; once you've written all over this copy and torn out some of the summary pages to keep close to your heart, you can always pop out and buy another one can't you? Or take a click route into the Amazon website. If you are based in the UK you can get a special deal via my website at www.cambridge-associates.co.uk

The overall message that I am trying to impress you with is a very simple one. Here is my two-minute message for this book; it's a two-minute message about the relevance and value of the two-minute message process. Phew!

Whatever your line of business, I'll bet that your customers are very busy people with many demands on their time. It is very important you have a good sales story to tell your customers and prospects, but that alone won't guarantee that you will get the time you need to tell it.

The Cambridge Associates' Two-Minute Message process is a tried and proven way of arousing your customer's curiosity and interest in what you have to say. Whatever you are 'selling', that's the start that you will need. It will also help you to put over your sales story, or to position the purpose and value of your organisation in the most compelling and most effective way. Guaranteed.

TODAY'S BUSINESS ENVIRONMENT

This book explains the TMM process and shows you how and where you can use it. It contains many examples from real life that you can adapt for your own use. I encourage you to read on.

The next section of the book puts the Two-Minute Message process into a 'real' context. Having done that, the remaining sections explain the process in some detail so you are able to apply it to your business situations. At the end of the book, you'll find a quick reference summary that you can use as an 'aide memoire', and some appendices with numerous examples.

Our TMM process will help you with your customer contact work, but it isn't the latest version of some magical snake oil. It won't make life 'easy' and it won't change the fact that effective communicating can be challenging and difficult.

It won't turn a complex challenge into a trivial one. Practise will turn it into a manageable one. And one that you will relish and profit from.

2
THE TALE OF TOMMY

WHAT THIS SECTION IS ALL ABOUT

This section of the book tells the story of Tommy, an enthusiastic, ambitious and energetic young sales representative who is keen to succeed. Just like many of the readers of this book, I'm sure.

It tells the story of how Tommy struggles through his business week trying to make best use of his time, without the benefit of a two-minute message.

Although this is written as a parody, a kind of fable, you will notice how the TMM technique could have helped Tommy in a variety of situations. I would bet that you recognize a few of them.

TOMMY GETS READY

This was a critical week for Tommy. He had some important meetings set up with his prospective clients, and he was determined to use this time to close some major sales.

He had spent the weekend putting his sales story together and his computer laptop presentation looked pretty good, even though he said so himself. Actually, his family thought so too, although there were quite a few bits that they couldn't understand.

"It's very pretty daddy," Tommy's young daughter was most enthusiastic about it. "Especially that bit where all those coloured arrows come zooming in and the music starts to play."

Tommy liked that bit too.

He knew that just having a slick presentation wasn't enough. Or even a 'pretty' one. On his sales training courses he had learned how important it was to build his sales story around the customer's business needs.

"Customer needs are very important." Tommy's sales training instructor was always quite adamant about this. "And you need an effective questioning technique to discover them. The wonderful features of your solution are worth nothing, unless they are put in the context of customer needs."

The trainer's big red moustache bristled with emphasis whenever he said this.

And he said it an awful lot.

THE 'INTRODUCTORY SUMMARY' SITUATION

For his first sales call of the week, Tommy had a meeting with the boss of a large organisation. He had done a good job in arranging this meeting. Or so he kept telling everyone.

"Persistence and charm," he told the rest of his sales colleagues, "use plenty of that and you can get past any secretary who is hell bent on protecting her boss's diary."

Tommy was telling a little white lie with this story, but no matter, no one would care about that when he brought in the big order. Actually it was quite a big white lie; the meeting had been agreed during a business luncheon involving the customer executive and Tommy's boss's boss.

THE TALE OF TOMMY

The customer had probably agreed to the meeting out of courtesy (or due to an excessive intake of wine) but nevertheless, Tommy intended to take full advantage of the situation.

Tommy had done lots of homework for this meeting (that was another good point he had picked up from the big man with the bristling red moustache). He had worked out the questions that he wanted to ask and he had written them down. He was word perfect with them and so he wouldn't need to read from his list.

"Make it a natural conversation, not an interrogation," his tutor had taught him, "once you get the client talking, you can go with the flow."

Tommy arrived early for his appointment. He had allowed himself some time to sit in the reception area and to watch the various comings and goings. He flicked through some of the literature on the reception table and made a few extra notes to his questions. Tommy smiled to himself. 'Another good tip from my sales training,' he thought.

Tommy felt confident as he was led into the executive office. He enjoyed these moments and the tingle of excitement that these situations always gave him.

After they had shaken hands and sat down around the shiny mahogany executive desk, the big Boss man looked across at Tommy. "OK young man," he said, "why don't you start by telling me what this meeting is all about and what value you think you can offer me?"

Tommy felt slightly taken aback by this statement; the briefing he had got from his manager after the customer luncheon hadn't prepared him for such a blunt opening gambit. Tommy glanced at his notes to remind himself of his first planned question. He knew it anyway, but the notes acted as their usual safety belt.

"You won't need to read your notes," his tutor had told him, "but you'll feel secure by having them to hand." "Well," Tommy started off, "I wonder if you could tell me about your debt collection process. What are the main problems that you get?"

"All in good time Sonny, all in good time," the boss man said, "that's a good question and we'll come back to it. But first I need to be happy about your PVC." Tommy's mind raced, and before he could pretend that he understood, the customer executive continued, "I'm talking about your purpose, your value and your credibility. Tell me what you might be able to offer me that would give me some benefit, and why *your* company is the one that I should be dealing with."

'Aha,' Tommy thought, `this is now right up my street, I can show him the presentation I've prepared.' Tommy clicked his laptop computer and began to talk about his opening visuals.

"Hold it a moment," the customer boss man interrupted. "You are misunderstanding me. I don't want to see your fancy slides or hear your lengthy sales presentation just yet, I want to hear your two minute summary version."

"Two minute version?" Tommy was puzzled. "I've planned this presentation to last fifteen minutes," he said, "well within our allotted time for this meeting."

"I allowed you twenty minutes assuming that this meeting would be a good use of my time," the boss man replied, "I'm a very busy man so I want to know how this meeting will benefit *me* before I let you start trying to sell me things."

Tommy's mind was racing. He could feel the adrenaline pumping round his system. At least he assumed it was adrenaline. The customer executive smiled at Tommy.

THE TALE OF TOMMY

"Listen son," he said, "think of it as telling me a joke, only I want to know your punchline before you start. Then I will know if it is really worth spending some time to hear the whole joke in more detail."

Tommy never got to ask his questions. He flummoxed and he flustered as he tried to make his point succinctly.

The big boss man was very polite. "Well, we've probably got to leave it there for the moment." He looked at his watch.

"Perhaps we can talk about it in more detail another time," he said, "I'll think about what you have told me and I'll be in touch."

But they both knew he didn't really mean it.

TOMMY'S FIRST LESSON

A TMM synopsis is your 'introductory summary'

THE TALE OF TOMMY

THE 'ELEVATOR CHALLENGE'

After a restless night, Tommy is scheduled to make a sales presentation to another important client.

This time he is convinced that everything will turn out OK. Nothing could possibly go wrong. How could it? He had prepared and rehearsed this presentation, but he hadn't learnt it as a script or anything daft like that.

"Make it sound off the cuff," his old tutor used to say, "even though it won't be." The sales trainer tutor certainly practised what he preached. Tommy had heard him churn out the same old jokes and anecdotes many times.

Tommy had done his research for this meeting. He knew that there would be a dozen people in the audience, and that he had twenty minutes to present his case. He had also been told that the customer people would hold back questions until he had finished his presentation.

"We prefer to hear the whole story before we ask any questions about it." Tommy was delighted when the meeting organiser told him that.

"It's the way that we like to do things round here," she said. "If you stick to your twenty minute slot, it will give us five or ten minutes to ask any questions that we might have."

'Great,' thought Tommy, 'that puts me in control.' His sales training tutor would be pleased.

"Get yourself in control of the questioning process." The sales training tutor would wave his arms around like a windmill whenever he made this point. "And then you won't be faced with silly interruptions that can knock you off your stride."

THE TWO MINUTE MESSAGE

Tommy knew that he had a good case to present. He expected that one or two people would argue with it, but he had anticipated all of the obvious objections and he planned to knock them on the head during his presentation. He was in good shape. He believed in what he was going to say and that was half the battle.

"Belief is very important," something else the man with the red moustache said many times, "if you don't look as if you believe in what you are saying then don't expect the audience to get excited. Even if they don't buy from you, they must see you as a sincere business person offering sound solutions and advice."

Tommy was pleased with himself. He had worked hard to fix this meeting and he knew that there was a quite a lot of interest in his presentation. Tommy smiled and nodded to the people as they came into the room and sat down. He chatted to some of them briefly and he introduced himself to others he hadn't met.

"Get comfortable with your audience," his tutor would say, "it is important that both you and they are relaxed. Take any opportunity to speak to them before you start your presentation."

Tommy could see the sense of what he had been taught. A few words beforehand always helps to break the ice and settle the butterflies in the tummy.

Tommy had already made sure that his laptop was plugged in and the projection kit worked well. He was tempted to check it once more, but he settled for a brief shuffle through his note cards.

"Shall we start then?"

Tommy was startled by the voice from the audience. He looked up at the man who had asked the question.

THE TALE OF TOMMY

"Perhaps we should we wait until everyone is here" he replied. The lady boss hadn't turned up yet and Tommy was very keen that she should hear what he had to say. She was the real decision maker after all.

Tommy looked nervously at his watch. He knew that he should have started his presentation a minute ago and he didn't want the audience to get restless.

"Never keep them waiting," his tutor had told him, "your customers are very busy people so you must appreciate the time they have given you. Always make sure that you start on time and that you finish a few minutes early. Your audience will appreciate it"

"Sorry I'm a few minutes late." Tommy was relieved when the lady boss walked in. Now he could stop fiddling with his notecards and get on with his presentation.

"Unfortunately, I can't stay for the presentation." Tommy gulped with dismay when she dropped her bombshell. "But don't worry," she smiled at him, "I know you've put a lot of work into this morning's event and I'm keen to hear your conclusions. Walk me to my car and give me a brief summary."

The lady boss turned to the group, "I'll just borrow him for five minutes then he's all yours," she said, "get yourselves a coffee or tea in the meantime."

As they travelled down in the elevator, the lady boss asked Tommy to summarise his presentation. Tommy felt lost without his laptop. He had planned his story around his visual aids and he felt helpless without them. He flustered and floundered and he started to describe the content of his presentation.

THE TWO MINUTE MESSAGE

"There's no need to tell me your agenda," she said, "I'm not interested in how you intend to structure your story, I just want a précis of what you will be saying. What's the bottom line of all this work you've been doing?" The journey was less than a minute but it felt like a lifetime to Tommy. For one crazy minute he considered hitting the emergency alarm and stopping the elevator mid floor. That would give him plenty of time to tell his story; there was so much he <u>could</u> say, but he couldn't work out where to start.

"I'd planned a twenty minute presentation," he said as they reached the ground floor, "it is very difficult to summarise it in a few words." The lady boss looked at him. "Well, don't worry," she said, "you get back to the people upstairs, we'd better not keep them waiting. Perhaps I'll try to get the gist of your story from one of them." She smiled at Tommy as the doors closed on him. She had pressed the button to send him back upstairs.

Damn, thought Tommy. It wouldn't be problem presenting his case if he was allowed his original allocated time, but one minute! The lady boss would hear a version of his story from someone else, but Tommy knew that he had missed a great opportunity. He wished he could have crystallised his big presentation into an effective synopsis.

TOMMY'S SECOND LESSON

A TMM synopsis gives you your 'elevator presentation'

THE 'SET PIECE' STORY

Tommy is in a meeting with his boss and some important clients. The clients were passing through town so they had agreed to meet in an airport hotel. It was a couple of hours before the clients had to catch their plane, so they had plenty of time for this meting.

Tommy was delighted that things were now starting to look up. He was getting rather fed up with people wanting him to condense his story - why couldn't they have the courtesy to let him tell it his own way and in his own time?

The customer people were looking rather dazed as Tommy's Boss droned on about the significance of transmission protocols and network speeds. "So the file sharing process enables the access routines to operate in conjunction with all the network protocols without any default..."

"Sorry, you've lost me there," one of the customer executives chipped in, "what's the relevance of all this technical wizardry and how will it help me?"

Good question thought Tommy. He picked some fragmented mint from the back of his mouth. He had lost the thread of the conversation and couldn't see what his Boss was getting at. He reached across the table for some mints. It always amused him how hotels assumed that business people would have an insatiable desire for peppermint and an unquenchable thirst for orange squash, lime juice and fizzy water. "Tommy, why don't you take that one, it's more up your field." Gee thanks Boss, thought Tommy swallowing his mint.

"Well," he gulped, "our proposed system is built around self-diagnostic procedures and our service support processes." Tommy started to stress the key benefits of his proposals. It wasn't what his Boss had been talking about but it was a critical point to get across.

THE TALE OF TOMMY

"Yes, yes, we've heard all that theory," the client managing director interrupted Tommy, "not that I understand it, mind you. And I certainly don't understand what is so special about it."

"Well, the exciting thing is that your people can diagnose a potential problem ahead of time and our remote call centres can talk them though the repair procedures step by step."

Tommy deliberately paused to let the dramatic significance of this point sink in.

"It doesn't even matter what country you could be calling from, because we can funnel the incoming calls to appropriate language skill groups," he went on. Tommy was enthusiastic about this subject and he knew it very well. "Our aim is to be the number one service provider in the world," he said. "We have built this concept into our company mission statement and our training programmes. All of our people now carry a wallet sized card to remind them of this."

That will show them how serious we are about being a world class organisation, he thought.

"Well ain't that just bully for you."

Tommy's sixth sense told him that the client's managing director hadn't appreciated the full value of what he had just said. "No really, this is extremely interesting," Tommy felt compelled to generate an enthusiastic reaction. "We have an on line diagnostic capability built into every one of our systems so each of our seventeen UK service centres can log on to them automatically." That was the clincher, Tommy thought, now for a bit of icing on the cake, "and by the way," he added, "it's a similar story right across the globe."

"Well it all sounds very Arthur C. Clarke to me."

This wasn't the reaction that Tommy wanted; he had hoped that the client executive would have been more impressed.

"We're a simple organisation," the executive continued, "we aren't technical boffins and I don't think we need anything as complicated as that."

Tommy was beginning to feel rather frustrated. "Look," he said, "I've got some slides here, I can show you how it all works." He pulled a demonstration binder from his briefcase.

"I think I can help you here."

Tommy paused and turned towards the client's technical director. Everyone did. This was a man who rarely spoke but when he did, it always made good sense.

"As we expand," the technical director said, "it is critical that we can guarantee the information flow between the point of sale and our order

THE TALE OF TOMMY

fulfilment process. Our business depends on it. This flow of information is just as vital to us as the flow of money, so our information systems must be absolutely foolproof."

Everyone nodded and murmured agreement. This was a point that wasn't in any dispute.

"And that's what we get with this new approach," the technical director went on, "the impressive thing about this system is that we don't have to be experts. Fault detection happens automatically, and the number of service centres means that any help we might need is never more than a stone's throw away. I'm all for it."

Tommy was delighted that at least one person in the assembled group had understood the fluency of his argument and could see the sense of it. It was a damned good overview though, better than he had done.

Tommy made a mental note to write it down when he had a spare moment.

TOMMY'S THIRD LESSON

A TMM synopsis gives you your set piece message

THE TALE OF TOMMY

THE PRESENTATION BUILDER

Tommy has been asked to prepare a thirty-minute presentation for tomorrow's client meeting. He knew the subject very well and he could see that this was a great opportunity for him to impress a senior customer audience.

"Remember that when you present to your client you have a sales opportunity." Tommy wished that he had a pound for every time the big man with the red moustache said this to his students. "You might not be selling a product, " he would say, "but you have a golden chance to sell your personal value and that of your organisation."

Tommy never really understood what the big man meant by the words 'golden chance' but, whatever it was, he wasn't going to let it slip by. It sounded too good to miss.

'If I get the presentation material sorted out pretty quickly,' he thought, 'I will have plenty of time to plan my script and rehearse the presentation until I am fluent.'

Tommy remembered that Charlie had done quite a few presentations on this topic so he called him on the telephone. If he could use some of Charlie's material it would give him the time he needed to get his lines worked out. "Look in my desk drawer," Charlie said, "second drawer down, left hand side. You'll find a couple of presentations I've done in the last three months; they worked very well for me. They're old technology style presentations I'm afraid, I never got the hang of all this fancy computerised stuff, but you should find everything you need in my overhead transparency folder."

Tommy started to convert some of Charlie's ideas into computerised PowerPoint slides. He intended to give the client an unforgettable audio-visual experience.

THE TWO MINUTE MESSAGE

"I can pump some life and colour into this material," Tommy muttered to himself as he put the computer software through its paces. Charlie's presentation material contained masses of good information, but the supporting visual aids were as dull as ditchwater. Lists of bullet points to prompt the presenter.

"Remember that the audience members own the visual aids." At first, Tommy had struggled to see the significance of his tutor's statement but his tutor's explanation had made it clear.

Think of your visual aids as adding value for the audience. They reinforce your message and help them to understand the points you are making. They might also help to keep you on track, but *that isn't their main purpose*. That's what your notes are for."

Tommy was pleased with his first half dozen slides, they were works of art compared to Charlie's original material, but he was aware that time was slipping by. "Don't keep reinventing the wheel." This was another good point from his sales training tutor. "Learn from your experiences and build on the work that other people have done."

THE TALE OF TOMMY

"Hey, what am I doing?" Tommy thought suddenly, "do I really need to create all these slides from scratch?"

He recalled the presentations that Katrina had done on this topic. They were lively pieces of work and she always seemed to get a good result. Tommy knew that Katrina would have lots of good presentation material set up on her laptop computer. If he could get her material he wouldn't have to spend time translating Charlie's stuff.

Tommy glanced at his watch. It was getting late but it wouldn't be too late to call Katrina. It never was. She was an energetic girl but Tommy reckoned she would have finished greasing her motorbike nipples by now.

"Yes, I've done lots of presentations on that subject," she told him, "stand by and I will email you all my PowerPoint slides."

Hours later Tommy stared at the material he had downloaded and collated together. It was all very good stuff but it seemed as if he had enough content for a two day seminar on the subject. If he flicked through the presentation slides without saying a word Tommy knew that it would take much more time than he had been allowed.

Tommy felt depressed and wondered how on earth he could say all that he wanted to say in only half an hour. There had to be an easier way. It shouldn't be this difficult to put a presentation together and it shouldn't take this long.

TOMMY'S FOURTH LESSON

A TMM synopsis should be your presentation *start* point

THE TALE OF TOMMY

THE LESSONS FOR TOMMY (and for all of us)

If the TMM fairy really existed (and who dares say she doesn't?), I wonder what she would tell Tommy. If she were to let him reprise his week 'Groundhog Day' style, what would she ask him to do differently?

She would probably say something along the lines of 'whatever your story, however simple or complex it might be, you need a two minute message for it'. No surprises in that, you might think, given the title of this book.

As a businessman I can recall being invited to social and sporting events with my suppliers. These were designed to help us get to know each other and to do some business 'bonding'. Whatever that might mean.

It always surprised me that whenever I asked the 'what does your organisation do?' type of question, it seemed to cause problems or create suspicion. I could see people thinking 'why is he asking that, it's obvious, what's the trick here?' There was no 'trick' to what I was trying to do. I was just making polite social conversation and it seemed a fair enough question. It was giving my hosts the chance to say something memorable and persuasive, and to impress me in some way.

When someone answered my question, more often than not I would get a very long and boring answer full of jargon and phrases that I couldn't understand. Sometimes (and here's the surprising bit), my host would make some comment about 'not wanting to mix business and pleasure' and change the subject.

This seemed like a lost opportunity, I didn't want to be bombarded with a long sales pitch of course, but a good TMM could have impressed me. The fact that the salesman ducked the question surprised me and made me wonder about the seriousness of the organisation that wanted to do business with me.

So you need some good set-piece TMMs about your role and your value.

And that's not just me talking, the TMM fairy says it too.

You need messages in varying levels of detail. Firstly to arouse interest, then to summarise your value and finally, to present your case in detail. A kind of 'message cascade'.

This situation is analogous to good journalism. The headline attracts you to the article; it helps you decide whether or not it'll be worth reading. That's your interest arousing TMM, the top layer of the cascade.

The opening paragraph of the article should give you an overview of what it is about and tell you the angle that the reporter is taking. That's the middle layer.

Finally there is the article itself which should live up to the promise of the previous two layers of the 'cascade'.

Regrettably, I have to tell you that the TMM fairy can't let Tommy reprise his week (she's far too busy elsewhere), but she can help you to learn from Tommy's experiences and avoid the same pitfalls.

She's instructed me to tell you to read on.

3

THE TWO MINUTE MESSAGE CONCEPT

We have used the phrase 'two-minute message' to describe the pre-planned synopsis that could have helped Tommy with his various challenges. You might have recognised some of these situations and although Tommy isn't a real person, I suspect that there's a bit of him in every one of us.

The rest of this book will help you to exploit the opportunities that he faced.

Each of Tommy's situations was a significant opportunity: A face to face call on a senior executive, the chance to summarise a business case for the client's CEO, answering a question of detail in a meeting and preparing an important presentation. Good salesmen often say that they would die for opportunities like these; they seek them out. You don't want to die (in a theatrical sense) when you meet them.

A TMM synopsis is the ideal starting point for any sales story or intended persuasive argument. It will help you to keep focus while you add the necessary detail you need to achieve your intended objective. Assuming of course that you have one.

"I don't need a specific objective when I talk to customers," a salesman once told me, "I bring as wide a range of topics as I can into the conversation, and I spot those that seem to strike a chord."

To be fair to this salesman, he was pretty good at doing this. Perhaps he could spot a gleam in the eye, a twitch in the leg, the flare of a nostril or some other neurolinguistical sign that would go unnoticed with most of us lesser mortals. But it all seemed a bit hit and miss to me and, come to think of it, this approach only worked with people he knew really well, never with strangers.

So there has to be a more reliable technique to 'striking that chord' with the customer and gaining the attention that you seek.

That's where the TMM technique comes in. So let us now examine the four main uses of a TMM.

USING A TMM TO AROUSE INTEREST IN A NEW TOPIC

This is probably the main application for a TMM and it is especially valuable when trying to make contact at a senior business level.

THE TWO MINUTE MESSAGE CONCEPT

Many of the sales training courses that I attended focused on developing expert questioning techniques and the skill of probing the customer for information. This would help us to identify the customer's issues and problems, and to unearth the painful implications of not sorting them out.

We were then taught to show how our solution could remove this pain and give the customer some benefit and value as a result.

That approach is very valid and I'm not knocking it, but sales people cannot presume that their clients will have the time, or inclination, to indulge them in this questioning process for the sake of it, however skilful they might be. This is especially true at a senior business level.

As a salesperson, you must be pro-active. You must initiate conversations that add value for the customer and aren't just intended to get information for yourself. It is up to you to identify appropriate topics to discuss. You will often spot opportunities to interest your customers in additional products or services, and unless you capture their attention straight away, that moment will be lost.

And it is important that you make the right impression. I don't know who coined the phrase, 'you only get one chance to make a first impression', but there's a lot of truth in that statement.

THE TMM AS A 'SET-PIECE' MESSAGE

In the book 'The Northbound Train', Karl Albrecht describes how a business should have a clear vision of the direction it must take to succeed. He uses the train analogy to describe the direction of the business and its speed and momentum in that direction.

This analogy can work just as well for a company division, a team and a department.

Wherever you fit, you should know your purpose and your direction, and you should be able to put that over concisely and with some passion.

This is one set piece message that you must be comfortable with. It should not only 'position' the role and value of your company (or business function), it should entice the audience to want to know more.

What it is that makes your 'Northbound Train' unique? Perhaps it's the speed, or perhaps it's the variety of onboard services. Or maybe it's the ancillary things that customers can pick up along the way.

There are four questions that business people should know about their company, and about the division or team they work in.

1. What we offer (business we are in and solutions we offer)
2. To whom we offer it (the nature of our clients)
3. Where we operate (scope, geography, niches, sectors)
4. Our overall purpose (value to the client, value to ourselves)

The answer to each of these questions isn't just a factual statement, (although you might want to start by agreeing the 'facts'). Every answer should be full of persuasion. Every answer should stress your competence, your strength and your uniqueness.

A tall order huh?

I'm not talking here about set presentations or advertising copy (important though both these things are). The set piece messages that I have described need to become ingrained into our everyday business conversations. We should use them to start debates and to answer questions. Getting back to the 'Northbound Train' analogy, people may not want to board our train at every stop, but they should be in no doubt as to its goal, its direction and the potential value of the journey with us.

THE TWO MINUTE MESSAGE CONCEPT

In our work with start up ventures and new initiatives, we ask our clients to prepare a compelling positioning statement. This is a simple (but not simplistic) summary of the reason that the business exists and the market opportunities it intends to exploit.

If you haven't got a two-minute message that does this for your business, build one as soon as you can.

There are other set piece messages of course, depending on your line of work. Summaries of your product capabilities, the quality of your customer service, the merits of a particular technology and so on.

Sometimes you will deliver a set-piece message in 'reaction' mode, i.e. in response to a customer initiative. Other times you could be saying your piece to create a good impression, or to prevent a problem developing.

I read somewhere that Mark McCormack, the international sports promoter insists that each of his account executives keeps a set of 'accomplishment files.' These are lists of every good thing that the organisation has done for each of its clients.

In McCormack's line of work, a typical entry would describe a luncheon that he had organised between the client executive and a famous golfer. Or perhaps providing tickets for a major sporting event.

These 'accomplishment files' help McCormack to remind his customers of the real value that he is providing. They are the basis of some very effective 'set piece' TMMs.

If you work in a business where you charge a premium price, the many good things that you do as part of your 'added value', can fade into the background and get forgotten. That is unlikely to happen with your price differential, so your challenge is to keep your added value in the forefront of your customer's mind.

I had an IBM colleague who was very good at doing this. He could even make a virtue from a problem.

"Everyone knows that there will be problems from time to time," he told me, "Convincing my customers that we can handle these problems gives them reassurance in my company".

Every so often, he and his team collated a summary of all the support activities and good-news items that were part of their day to day operations.

"If I use this information wisely," he said, "I can remind the customer executives what they are really getting for their money. More importantly, it makes them understand what they would lose if they gave their business to a lower cost supplier. My clients aren't buying products from me; they are buying reassurance and peace of mind."

Putting these points across succinctly is what a set piece TMM is all about.

THE TMM AS A PROMOTIONAL LETTER

A TMM is usually a spoken message but it can also be written down. A brief introductory letter can set the scene for an important telephone call or meeting. But it must be <u>brief</u>; preferably no more than a single page.

'Aha,' I hear you say, 'one page - that's easy.' But I'm afraid it isn't; it will take time to do properly. You may have heard the story about the salesman who said to his customer, "I'm sorry that I've written you such a long letter, I didn't have time to write a short one".

A succinct TMM letter won't guarantee success, but it will increase your chances. Almost everybody will read a single page letter in its entirety, but that isn't necessarily the case for a longer document. I'm talking here about the 'black-marks-on-white-paper' documents. Remember those?

THE TWO MINUTE MESSAGE CONCEPT

But the same argument applies to e-mail correspondence. Get your point across before the recipient has to start scrolling down. Or at least make him or her want to scroll down.

One old fashioned English CEO I worked with was new to electronic communications and didn't realise that you could scroll down. I wonder how many compelling sales arguments he missed.

I've heard people argue against sending introductory letters. "It will brief your customer people beforehand," they say, "there will be no surprises and when you meet, they will know how to argue against you."

In my book (and this is my book), that would be a wonderful state of affairs. We would be into a meaningful discussion straight away.

"There are many good reasons for sending a letter ahead of an important call," my old tutor used to say. "It is courteous, it is professional and it brings your name to their attention. These letters are a form of free advertising. They get put on file and circulated for other people in your customer organisation to see."

In this email driven world of correspondence, however, it makes good sense to write your important TMM letters on your formal, posh paper with your letterhead on display. These documents build a physical record of your value, and your customer is more likely to file a piece of correspondence than an email. Maybe times will change, but I recommend that your clients have a physical record of your propositions and the benefits that you bring.

A neighbour of mine, who ran his own business from home, confirmed my thinking. "It has suddenly dawned on me," he said, "If my main client contact were to leave, there is very little information about me on the customer files."

He, like most of us, had thrown himself into the convenience and efficiency of email. And it's potential anonymity. It probably isn't as anonymous as my friend was worried about, and getting less so, but it is worth regarding some of your good TMM letters as potential brochures; as things you want lots of people to see. So perhaps put them on your website. And consider sending hard copies for some of them.

TMM letters can be difficult to write (hence my earlier quotation about apologising for a long letter), but they are well worth the effort.

Later in this little gem of a book I'll show a structure that will help you.

USING A TMM TO PLAN A MAJOR PRESENTATION OR EVENT

The TMM process will also help you to construct the skeleton of an important presentation. One of the main challenges of doing this is deciding what to include in the presentation, and what to leave out. We saw how Tommy decided to take advantage of previous presentation materials. That's fine in principle, but how often have we seen salespeople leafing through old presentation material and shuffling bits of them together to create a new one?

Or more to the point, how often have we done that ourselves?

Every presentation should be built from a two minute version. If you learn nothing else from this book it will have been time well spent for you. But only if you put it into practice of course.

One well-known presentation training organisation refers to this kind of synopsis as 'the red thread of the story.' It is the essence of the message. A good 'red-thread' synopsis will keep you focussed on your presentation objective and it will help you add the necessary amount of detail that you need to achieve it. And no more.

THE TWO MINUTE MESSAGE CONCEPT

This synopsis will also give you the TMM that you will need to get your client interested in hearing your presentation in the first place. And if you find yourself travelling in an elevator with a senior executive, you will have the presentation synopsis that our young friend Tommy lacked.

So with a good TMM synopsis you can kill two birds with one stone.

Clever eh?

4
BUILDING YOUR TMM

This section of the book gives you a 'recipe' approach to building your two-minute message. It will take time for you to work out the precise words and phrases that you will use, especially if you are preparing a TMM letter, but this step by step approach will help you to get the structure of your message sorted out very quickly.

THE 'OATS' MNEMONIC
This shows the four key stages in building your TMM.

- OBJECTIVE
  Defining the outcome that you want to achieve
- AUDIENCE
  Identifying your targeted person (or persons)
- THEMES
  Selecting the main points of your message, i.e. the 'themes' that will help you to achieve your objective.
- SYNOPSIS
  Having done the above preparatory steps, you then put these themes into a predefined sequence that will give maximum effectiveness.

You follow that sequence of steps to build your TMM.

DEFINING YOUR 'SMART' OBJECTIVE
In his book, *The Seven habits of Highly Effective People',* Stephen Covey describes the concept of *'beginning with the end in mind.'* That approach applies to the two-minute message process. In other words, your first task is to define your objective. This is the outcome you want

from your TMM - the clearly defined state that you want to reach as a result of having delivered it. A good objective is often referred to as 'SMART.' This acronym describes the attributes of a good objective.

SPECIFIC
It is directed at a specific person (or refers to a specific project).

MEASURABLE
You have defined the end result in such a way that you can 'measure' achievement in a 'yes we have,' or 'no we haven't,' binary sense.

ACHIEVABLE
You can see how the objective can be achieved, given the resources that you have identified.

RELEVANT
The objective makes good sense and is line with your wider goals.

TRACKABLE
You know how you can measure progress towards completing your objective.

'Making a good impression' is a very worthy intention, but it isn't a well expressed objective; it doesn't meet our 'SMART' criteria. For instance, how would you track it and how would you know when you had achieved it?

If you were setting an objective for how you would use a TMM to open your sales call, something like the following statement might be nearer the mark.

'To have established our potential value to the extent that the client is genuinely willing to continue the discussion.'

BUILDING YOUR TMM

This is an improvement on the original statement although the phrase *'to have established our potential value'* is rather vague, and you would need a more specific focus for your introductory message.

On the positive side, the latter part of the objective statement, *'..the client is genuinely willing to continue the discussion'*, gives a binary measure of success. You could judge whether or not you had achieved that situation.

There is another useful acronym that will help you remember the characteristics of a good objective. We invented this one within Cambridge Associates so it probably isn't as well known as 'SMART' (but it will be once this book appears on the best seller lists).

THE 'DRACHMA' DEFINITION OF A GOOD OBJECTIVE

Using this definition, a good objective should be each of the following:
DESIRABLE
You must want to do it, it is important for your 'success'
RESPONSIBILITY-BASED
It is line with your responsibilities and fits in with the wider aims of the business
ACHIEVABLE
You can see a way to achieving it and you have identified the resources needed to do so
CHALLENGING
It isn't easy; it should stretch you (and the business) and take things forward
HELPFUL
It is phrased in such a way that you (and others) can see how to go about it
MEASURABLE
It is time-stamped and you can see how you measure progress towards its achievement
ACCEPTED
You accept it willingly. In the case of job objectives, you are likely to have been party to its creation.

TMM OBJECTIVES VERSUS CAMPAIGN OBJECTIVES

The 'DRACHMA' acronym contains the same key characteristics as 'SMART', but it implies a hierarchy of objectives. This will be true in your line of business although it mightn't be expressed formally. Your function and your job objectives will relate to the wider needs of the business. As you achieve what you are setting out to do, you are helping the business to reach its goals. When you set an objective for your TMM, you will be doing so in the wider context of your sales campaign or any 'persuasive' campaign (i.e. one where you are trying to persuade your target audience to embark on a course of action).

It is important not to confuse your TMM objective with the overall objective of your sales campaign. Your campaign, for example, could be to sell a two million pound outsourcing contract, but winning that contract isn't the objective of your TMM. Your TMM would be intended to arouse the customer's interest in the concept of outsourcing to the extent that he is prepared to discuss it with you.

The TMM objective and the campaign objective are related. The TMM is the first milestone point en route to your final goal (your campaign objective).

By the way, if you are able to make a two million pound outsourcing sale in two minutes, throw this book away and get on with it.

In our example scenario, your TMM objective could be, 'to arouse the client's interest in the potential value of outsourcing, and to agree a meeting (involving appropriate parties) where we can discuss this in more detail.'

At the end of your TMM (and the discussion that follows it) you will have achieved your objective if you could say to your client, *'Thank you for our brief discussion. I will now arrange a forum where we can debate this in more detail and we can present our ideas to you. Perhaps a good first step would be for me to suggest an agenda and recommend who we invite to this forum.'*

Or words to that effect.

A sales (or 'persuasive' oriented) campaign could be defined as one that has the objective of convincing the target audience to embark on a course of action. This invariably means that you will be asking for some kind of resource, and that you want your target audience to accede to your request.

'Time' is one category of resource. By implication, your TMM is asking your target audience to surrender some of this resource in order to hear your story in more detail. In your overall sales campaign, you are likely to be seeking other types of resources.

A resource is a source of something of value to both the giver and the receiver of it. It isn't something you should expect to get lightly; you will have to justify why it should be given to you. Unless of course you are prepared to pay for it in some way.

You'll meet one or two new acronyms (or are they mnemonics?) in this book (and a few old friends). Here is one to help you identify the different categories of resource that you could be seeking.

THE FOUR 'M' DEFINITION OF RESOURCES

There are four major categories of resource.

MINUTES:
Time resources. Every minute that you take from the client is denying him (or her) a minute that could be allocated elsewhere. This is an underrated and very often abused resource. Very often we take it for granted that this resource is readily available. And, of course, there are direct and opportunity costs associated with this resource.
MANPOWER:
People resources, in terms of both numbers of people and particular skills that you might need.
MONEY:
Funding and budget allocation. Salesmen spend most of their waking hours chasing for more than their fair share of this resource.
MACHINERY:
This is a general category of resource, referring to facilities, equipment, materials, office space, and so on.

YOUR TARGET AUDIENCE
Having established your objective, the next step is to identify the target AUDIENCE for your message.

In truth, you would probably have a target audience in mind as you were thinking of your objective, but this process would ruin my OATS mnemonic!

So let us compromise and say that you do them in harmony.

'EXTERNAL AND INTERNAL' AUDIENCE CANDIDATES
These are your potential target 'customers', and I use the word 'customer' in its most general sense. Most of the time when you think of your customers, you will think of those people who pay for your products and services (these are the 'revenue generating' type of customer).

There are other people and functions on whom you are dependent, and to whom you have responsibilities that are not measured in revenue terms. There are times when you will need to engage their attention and persuade them to support you in some way. Your boss, your colleagues, people from other functions in your business and your suppliers, all fall into this category.

Perhaps you want them to support you, or agree to your business plan. Very often you will be trying to persuade them to give you some resources.

You should always plan your TMM for a specific audience, i.e. for a named individual.

It is better, for example, that you design your message for 'Paul Prentice, the Group Finance Director of Western Treaty plc', than design it for 'any finance director of a large plc.'

You could start on a general basis and tailor your message later, I suppose.

But it isn't the best way.

ANALYSING YOUR AUDIENCE

This is where I want you to analyse your audience's 'KAMA'. No, I'm not talking about some new mystical language. This is yet another useful mnemonic. This one stands for 'knowledge, attitude, motivation, action.'

The latter two letters (M and A) relate to the objective you have set for your TMM. You have defined the outcome that you want (that's the 'action' bit) and you need to motivate your target audience to agree to it.

The first two letters of this KAMA mnemonic refer to 'knowledge and attitude.' You will know, or you must 'best-guess', your target audience's knowledge of your topic and his or her attitude to it. This will guide the content and the tone of your message. What applies for one sales director could be inappropriate for another. Their jobs could be almost identical and they could have common issues, but their level of knowledge and their attitude should influence the direction and the tone of your message.

Hence my preaching about the importance of tailoring the message to a specific audience.

With your objective and your audience in mind, the next stage is to identify your key THEMES.

THE THEMES OF YOUR MESSAGE

These are the key points that you want your audience to remember. But you must be selective; saying too much can have a worse effect than saying too little. And you don't pick them randomly like matches from a street seller.

Remember the words of my old art teacher. In most situations, 'less' will be 'more'.

Likewise, if you swamp your client with too much detail and too many impressive statements, you will dilute the effectiveness of your message.

THEMES VERSUS FACTS

For any topic, there will be many true statements that you could make, many 'facts' that you could regurgitate. It is important that you select those points that are relevant to your audience and which will help you reach your objective.

I've stressed the importance of tailoring your message to your audience but there is *some* value in identifying some general themes that could apply to a particular message.

If, for example, you were preparing a TMM about a new product or service, you could identify themes like,
- how this service could help you to reach new markets
- how it could help you keep competition at bay
- how it could speed up your internal processes
- how it can cut costs out of your business
- how it will improve employee effectiveness
- how our product support processes work (and their value to you)
- our speed of delivery and the impact of this on your business
- the advantages of our unique technologies
- the benefits of our customer support processes

You can see already that this list of value statements could go on and on, and how we could be in danger of noting every known fact about our product, irrespective its relevance. There could be little point in promoting our ability to help the client reach new markets if we are talking to a finance director, who is obsessed with cutting costs.

So you must be selective.

Some years ago, I was advising a client who was trying to sell services to a UK Building Society. The sales team had put together a story that included lots of impressive statements about their organisation. Every one of these statements was true, but they weren't all helpful.

On the contrary, the many 'chest-beating' type comments were in danger of blurring the real message.

One client of mine referred to these as Muhammad Ali comments ('I am the greatest') and if you make too many of these, you could become viewed as being arrogant.

So be selective when choosing your themes (remember the phrase 'less is more') and make sure that they are relevant to your objective.

STRENGTHS AND 'UNIQUES'

You would probably want your TMM to highlight the strengths of your suggestion and the things that make it unique. But what do we mean by these words?

A 'strength' is something that you are good at. It is something that you or your organisation does very well, something you can be proud of perhaps.

Remember though, that there are some basic things that you must have in order to compete in your chosen market sector. It isn't a 'strength' that you can offer a support service for your products; it's a basic requirement. Without it you don't deserve to be in the marketplace. There may be some *aspect* of your approach to customer service that makes you special. The quality of what you do, for example. That could be a strength, especially if it puts you in the top echelon of service providers, but in this example it is the quality of your service that you feature as a strength, not the fact that you *offer* service.

There's an important difference. Without labouring the point too much (well only a little), imagine you were buying a motor car. If the salesman started telling you that the real 'strength' of a particular vehicle was the fact that it had four wheels complete with tyres, you'd think he was crazy. You'd begin to wonder what he had been smoking.

These things aren't 'strengths'; they are basic requirements. The fact that the wheels were of a particular brand of alloy and that the tyres had the latest super-grip capability to keep you secure in wet conditions, might be factors worth highlighting.

Let me digress slightly for a moment and make some comments about 'added value', a phrase that salespeople use a lot these days when talking about their 'strengths'.

The phrase 'added value' is part of today's sales language, but what does it really mean? To feel it in the way that our customers do, we need to understand where a basic service ends and additional value begins. Replace the word 'added' with the word 'additional' in the phrase, and we begin to get close to the mark.

In 'The Northbound Train', Karl Albrecht introduces the concept of a hierarchy of customer perceived value. He defines four levels of customer value - *Basic* (lowest level), *Expected, Desired* and *Unanticipated* (highest level). The model is cumulative; each level building on the one below it, so you cannot get to level two (for argument sake) until you have satisfied level one.

I applied this model in a client workshop and we fleshed it out in more detail. So here's the Albrecht/Freeman version:

1. *Basic Level* - The fundamentals of your customer service. For example, you must provide sound working mechanisms for customers to contact you. Making these work efficiently isn't *adding* value, it's fulfilling the basic requirements of doing business to the customer's satisfaction. Get these fundamental processes wrong and they will dominate every conversation you have with your client. Marketing people refer to these areas as 'moments of truth'.

2. *Expected Level* - This level of service is 'the norm'. It is what a customer expects his supplier to do. Look at us,' suppliers sometimes say, 'we answer eighty percent of incoming service calls in less that twenty seconds'. Or whatever.

   'Big deal,' the customers say. 'Isn't that what you are supposed to do? It's what you promised us when we signed the contract'

   So living up to expectations and meeting promises isn't <u>adding</u> value, it's doing what customers expect. Of course, it is important that you remind your customer how well you perform these functions - especially if your competition is struggling to do so. But remember; as a market matures and customer expectation increases many more things will become *'expected'*.

3. *Desired Level* - This is the first level of true added value (additional value). You can be proactive and offer facilities that your customers would like to have, but never thought to be possible. It is very important, however, that you set the right expectations, otherwise you could find yourself back to level one in no time.

4. *Unanticipated Level* - This is where you are truly proactive; you make your customers aware of new opportunities and you keep them abreast of technological and business developments. Albrecht uses the phrase 'giving the customer some surprises', but presumably not of the kind: 'Now there's a surprise, they've managed to deliver it on time for once!'

   I know what Albrecht is getting at but I prefer the phrase 'customer delight'. It's unambiguous.

Adding real customer value begins at category 3 and comes to life in category 4, but they won't get a look in unless the first two are in good shape. In your sales discussions, you must reinforce your basic capabilities (categories 1 & 2), but you should strive to reach a position where the higher categories dominate the debate. These are your real strengths.

Thank you for your indulgence, digression over.

So a strength is something beyond the basic requirements that makes your product 'fit for purpose'. It is something worth featuring because it adds credence to your claim. But it might not be unique; your competitors could have this attribute too. That shouldn't stop you identifying your strength and including it as an important theme in your message. A 'unique' is something that only you can offer, or something that you are best at doing.

Once again, of course, these wonderful facets about you or your products are only relevant if they offer a benefit to the client. You might be the world expert in origami, but if your client isn't interested in the art of paper folding, it will mean very little. Nothing in fact.

Taking a more realistic example, you could be the only organisation that has a sales office in Timbuktu, but that is somewhat academic as far as the Lower Puddleton Building Society is concerned (as far as I know).

TESTS FOR SELECTION
So how do you decide which 'themes' to include in your message? In my workshop sessions, very often something strange takes place when I set the group the task of identifying 'our strengths'. People find some hitherto missing verbal freedom and they start to let rip with every positive comment that they can think of.

Typically, there is masses of enthusiasm and lots of frantic scribbling, resulting in every possible known fact about the company and its products being displayed on flipcharts and whiteboards. And a few unknown ones as well. It's a great psychological release for the group, I'm sure.

Let me give you an important phrase to keep in the back of your mind whenever you try to identify your 'strengths'.

Better still, I suggest you write in your diary, enter it in your filofax, or key it into your laptop. I've got it scratched on my Elvis Presley pencil box. Here it is,

'A 'strength' is <u>only</u> a 'strength' if we can exploit it to achieve our objective.'

This phrase will help you filter out some 'strengths' which could be genuine statements of truth, but which are not relevant to your current TMM.

Ask yourself the question, 'could we exploit this (feature) to make our campaign objective more attainable?' The answer must be a resounding 'yes' for you to have identified a genuine strength that you can exploit to help you achieve your campaign objective.

Likewise a 'weakness' is only relevant if it genuinely inhibits your progress.

THE TMM BUILDING BLOCKS

So let us assume that you are clear about the topic you want to discuss and that you have a target victim in mind (sorry, I mean intended audience).

You know the outcome that you want and you have sorted out a list of the main points that you want to make.

You are now ready to construct your TMM.

THE TMM FOUR PART STRUCTURE

A good TMM has four components, constructed in the following sequence:
1. The audience context statement
2. Your key theme
3. Your supporting themes
4. Your closing statement

YOUR AUDIENCE CONTEXT STATEMENT (ACS)

The start point for every TMM is to set the scene from the customer's point of view. We call this the 'audience context statement.'

Every statement of value must be set in an audience context. That should be obvious but I'll repeat it with some emphasis,

'Every statement of value must be set in an audience context'

Excuse me for a moment while I scratch it on my pencil box.

You might be thinking 'so what's the big deal? If all of this is so obvious, why is he stressing it so much?'

Modern sales people talk about making 'value propositions' and 'value statements' to their clients. Both of these concepts are very good, but they must be set in an appropriate context. The truth is that a bold claim made out of context can seem arrogant, even when the claim could be justified.

'My double-glazing can reduce your heating bills by twenty percent.' We've all heard sales statements like that - and it might be a valid proposition of some value. As a statement it is probably true, but, in isolation, it is unlikely to make you want to pursue the offer. Perhaps I'm wrong. You might be the kind of person that is attracted to any apparent bargain. If so, please send me your contact details. Boy, have I got a deal or two for you. However, if the opening part of the conversation had raised the issue of heating costs, and if this was an issue that concerned you, then the proposition would have a better chance of arousing your interest.

The opening statement of your TMM (i.e. your audience context statement) should state something that is relevant to the recipient of the message. It should *not* say anything about you, your company or your products. The same rule applies to a written TMM. Your opening sentence, or paragraph, should set the scene for your message in customer terms. In both of these instances (a spoken or written TMM), I'm talking about situations where you are initiating the conversation and trying to arouse interest in your topic. If you are reacting to a direct question, the context could be self-evident but, even then, a brief context statement will make your message more relevant.

A good ACS will state an accepted (or likely) customer issue or business statement of fact, and its implications. It should be a statement that the recipient would agree to.

EXAMPLES OF AUDIENCE CONTEXT STATEMENT
- *'We are aware of your plans to ...'*
- *'In your line of business, Mr Customer, we have noticed that other organisations are reviewing the issue of ...'*
- *'The recent business articles on (something or other) are quite interesting, they point out that ......*
- *'Businesses like yours Mr Customer, are facing the challenges of expanding abroad into to new market areas ....'*
- *'Success in your marketplace depends on the quality of service that you give your customers and how well you can satisfy their demands ...'*
- *There seem to be a lot of new competitive threats in your line of business...'*

And so on.

Here are two statements taken from real life. You don't need to know the names of these organisations (although you might be able to guess their respective lines of business). Note these statements set the scene without mentioning 'us' – i.e. the name of the company concerned or its products or services.

Here's the first one:
'In an attempt to satisfy the world's increasing demands for energy, it's easy for companies to overlook the importance of plants and animals. But ignoring endangered species can be very costly. Lasting environmental damage and public outrage are the real business consequences of forgetting the small and the vulnerable'

No one can really disagree with that. It shouts out 'we are an energy company that cares'. I would add the word 'justifiable; in front of 'public outrage' to give it more impact, but they didn't ask my opinion.

That's their loss.

Look at this next one. It sets the scene by making a statement about technology.

'New technologies have given rise to unprecedented possibilities in every aspect of our lives. The application of these technologies to the HR function is leading to radical changes in the way in which this function is performed'

You could replace 'HR' in that statement with the name of almost any business function and the statement would be applicable.

The opening statement is very important. It creates the context for your message and makes it more valuable and relevant. Advertising companies write in this way instinctively. Your opening statement should be non-contentious (ideally) and one that the customer will accept readily, so there is no need for you to labour this part of your message. Using an audience context statement will set the scene for your 'value propositions' or whatever terminology you use to describe how wonderful you can be. And it will make one hell of a difference.

Trust me, I'm a doctor.

YOUR KEY THEME
This is the 'headline' of your message: It is the single point (of possibly many) about your company, yourself or your solutions that you want the customer to remember. If you could only make one point, this would be it.

You don't select this point at random, nor do you choose the most impressive item from your list of possible options. Your key theme should be the one that will help you to make the most progress towards achieving your objective. And it should be a logical extension of your audience context statement.

For example, consider a message that starts as follows:

'We have read about your ambitious plans to expand your business into to Europe and the demands that this will place on the local operations in each country.'

This goes slightly beyond a simple statement of context, the second half of the message draws out some implication or issue that the customer will have. That's good, but remember we want the customer to agree with our context statement (or at least not disagree with it) so make sure that you can justify any issue that you infer.

Given that ACS, your key theme should cite the main feature of your approach that could help the customer to do this.

'We have full support operations in each of these countries which we can co-ordinate from the UK. No one else can offer this level of support...'

Now I don't know if that point is any good or not, it's an academic example (actually it isn't, but I've neutralised it to protect the innocent). But it is a *relevant* theme; it addresses the issue raised in the audience context statement.

A different key theme could be less effective.

'We invest umpteen million pounds a year in research and development.'

This impressive statement might be absolutely true but it doesn't build on the audience context statement quoted earlier. It is a 'Muhammad Ali' claim, made in isolation.

So there are two questions you should ask about your key theme. There are two tests that you should apply to verify that you have chosen the most appropriate theme to spearhead your message.

1. Does this theme relate to my audience context statement? In other words, does it address the issue or implications that are contained within it?

2. If I lead with this theme, will it help me to achieve my objective?

WHY ONLY A SINGLE THEME?
That's a fair question; After all, there are many points that you probably could make. I'm asked that question quite a lot on my Two Minute Message Workshop sessions. (Hint, hint, book now while there are places available. Write to me at wdf@cambridge-associates.co.uk)

'Tell me, oh Great One,' a participant will say, 'I have two very good points that I want to make, why can't I use them both?'

It can be difficult to select a single theme, I grant you, and it isn't a disaster if you are unable to pick a main one, but it is an excellent discipline to try to do so. It forces you to tailor the message to your audience and to be crystal clear about your objective. Nine times out of ten when my workshop participants struggle to identify a single key theme, it is because either they are not clear about their objective or they haven't got a specific audience in mind.

But we sort it out in the end. Usually.

Think of it as like having a set of bow and arrows. You have the mechanism to fire your arrows and you have a loaded quiver to select from. These arrows represent your possible 'themes'. In this analogy all your themes are the same, so let's take it a stage further and imagine they are all different. Different sizes, different flights, different capabilities. Some might be designed to kill, some to send messages, some to light beacons and so on. Depending on your target (target audience) and what you are trying to do (your objective), you need to select the most appropriate arrow to fire first (you might not get a second chance). This is analogous to selecting your key theme.

Just think of what we could have done for Robin Hood.

YOUR SUPPORTING THEMES
This probably seems obvious. In seeking your key theme, you will have listed half a dozen or more pretty impressive statements. The supporting themes must be all the many other impressive points that were the rejected candidates for your key theme, mustn't they?

Not necessarily, we apply a bit more science than that. There are two types of supporting theme.

The first type adds credence to your key theme by providing supporting evidence to substantiate it. Client references are a good example of this type. If your key theme describes a feature of your product or service which can help your clients get new routes to market, a good supporting theme would be to comment on the number and types of business that are realising these benefits. Putting some proof in the pudding, so to speak.

You get credence by quoting specific names, 'we did this for client XYZ and they saved ....'. Don't forget too what you have done within your own organisation. Some people say that internal references add less impact than those that are client based. Maybe so, but don't underrate their value.

There will also be some valid themes which are unrelated to the key theme, but which could help the client to address the implied issues of the audience context statement. That's the second category of supporting theme.

We can usually find a home for some of our rejected key theme contenders in the 'supporting themes' category.

YOUR CLOSING STATEMENT
This statement should make a link back to your objective by making an appropriate suggestion or request.

'So you see Mr Customer, there are several areas where we could help you cut some of your costs. Can I suggest that we do some more work on this and present our findings to you?'

That is OK, but it could be strengthened. We might have let ourselves in for quite a bit of work without any real commitment from the customer. It can be easy for a customer to say 'yes' to your suggestion out of courtesy (or a desire to close the meeting!).

You can test the customer's commitment by asking for a further meeting and agreeing the agenda. Or by asking him/her to agree that you work alongside some customer staff to do your preparatory work.

If you are giving a set piece TMM in response to a question, you might feel that there isn't a need for much of a closing statement. Possibly so, but for each of your set pieces, think of the next logical steps. Is there a workshop or a seminar that you are running that could give your clients more information on the topic? Are there news articles or other pieces of literature that you could refer them to?

5
IDENTIFYING YOUR TWO MINUTE MESSAGE TOPICS

There will be some topics that you would like to discuss with your customers and there will be others that you could be expected to be asked about. Your customers are likely to want your opinions on your company's latest press release or product announcement, for example. If you are to get close to your customer and sell your value, then you must be able to make succinct and positive comments about the issues of the day.

You create value in the eyes of your customer when the benefits that you offer seem to outweigh the time, effort and costs of getting them. And in a competitive world, it is important that you offer the best value you can. In my experience, many salespeople undersell their total value: they focus on their proposed solutions but often miss out two other key aspects.

On our value-building workshops I make the analogy of a triple flavoured ice-cream cone. Think of a hot summer afternoon and the pleasure of clutching one of those triple cones with dollops of vanilla, strawberry and chocolate-chip ice cream.

In my analogy these three flavours represent the three key strands of value.

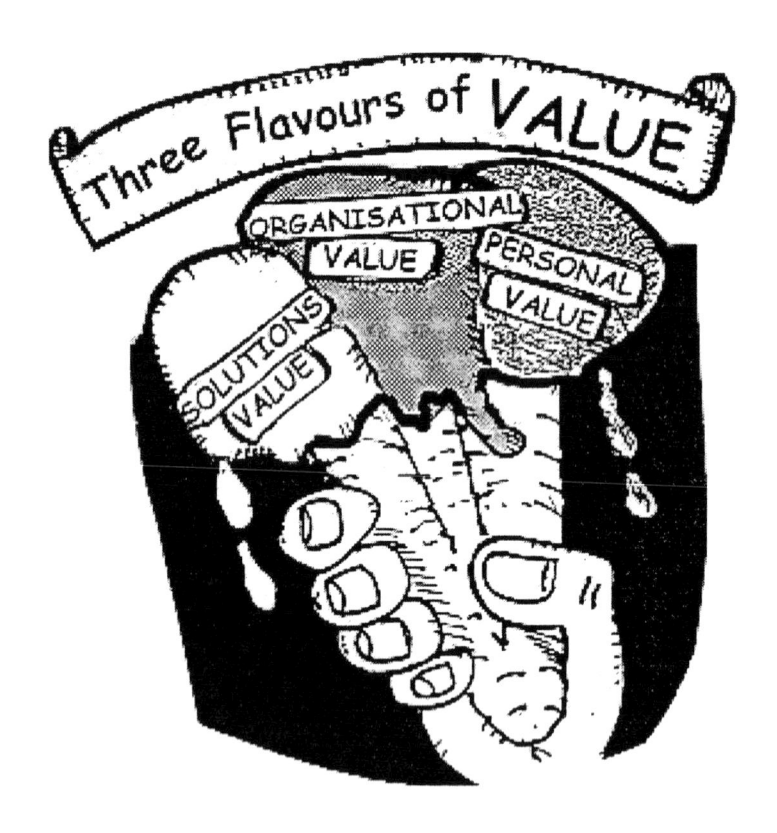

YOUR THREE STRANDS OF POSSIBLE VALUE

- PRODUCTS AND SOLUTIONS VALUE: This is the vanilla stuff; the net benefits that your customer will get from your products and services. Typical benefits are reduced costs, increased efficiency, improved routes to market and so on. The customer gets value when the benefits exceed the costs of ownership. This is familiar territory for all sales people so I'll say no more about this aspect.

- ORGANISATIONAL VALUE: Your customer could be facing business issues that your organisation understands very well. If your business has been successful in expanding abroad, downsizing, introducing home-working or whatever, you can apply that knowledge to your customer. As a consultant, I charge for such services but your 'company knowledge' could be part of the added-value of doing business with you. Come to think of it, it might be a damned good reason for the customer to want a relationship with you, even when he isn't in a buying mood.

Your customer base is another strand of knowledge you could exploit. You will know how other businesses and market sectors are tackling particular problems and, without breaking confidences, you could apply that knowledge too. We've gone beyond vanilla and my strawberry cone represents these aspects of added value.

- PERSONAL VALUE: Chocolate-chip ice cream is the clincher for me, it's that little extra touch that sways the balance and convinces me to buy. Your personal background, experiences and business contacts could add value to your customer's strategic debate. Think about your job role and those of your supporting account team members. What would the customer lose if these roles didn't exist? Conversely, what potential value do they add?

If you focus on solutions value only, then you could get dragged into a price debate. That's fine if you are a vanilla flavoured value business only. If you are in the added-value arena make sure that you sell your true and total value. You don't have to fill all three cones equally, but don't expect to win if you leave any of them empty.

Here are some examples, phrased as they were in real life on one of our TMM workshops sessions.

The titles of my examples might not set you on fire, but remember these are just working titles to get us started. They can be jazzed up later.

TOPIC EXAMPLES

PRODUCTS AND SOLUTIONS VALUE
- *'The unique benefit of (a particular product)'*
- *'The value and benefits that other clients get from our products and services'*
- *'How our offerings complement your current supplier's products'*
- *'The true costs of ownership'*
- *'Our outsourcing capabilities'*
- *'The added value benefit that your business will get, short term and long term'*
- *'How our proposition will improve your business 'scorecard''*

OUR ORGANISATIONAL VALUE
- *'Our company purpose, mission and vision and its relevance to our clients'*
- *'How our company's global strategy will help your business to expand abroad'*
- *'The relevance of our investments in research and development'*
- *'Our policies regarding joint ventures and partnership arrangements'*
- *'Our value in helping you cope with business change'*
- *'How our experiences (in a particular area) can help you'*

PERSONAL VALUE
- *'My job function and how it can benefit your business'*
- *'The added value you will get from our support resources'*
- *'The rationale of our latest reorganisation (and how this benefits our clients)'*
- *'The value of our specialist skills and functions'*

You will notice that the phrasing of many of these topic titles implies a benefit.

IDENTIFYING YOUR TMM TOPICS

Delivering an effective two minute message is much more than making a succinct statement to answer a question, or to state a case. It should be phrased to arouse interest, and to sell the benefit of yourself, your company and the services you offer. Possibly all three.

Try using these headings to identify your top three or four TMMs in each category. Don't worry too much about fitting your ideas into the correct category. The next section has expanded some of the category heading to help prompt your ideas, try filling it in.

MY LIST OF TWO MINUTE MESSAGE TOPICS

TMM TOPICS BASED ON THE VALUE OF OUR PRODUCTS / SERVICES AND OUR SPECIFIC PROPOSED SOLUTIONS

1._____
2._____
3._____
4._____

TMM TOPICS BASED ON THE VALUE OF OUR COMPANY (ORGANISATION, STRATEGIES, POLICIES) AND OUR INDUSTRY KNOWLEDGE

1._____
2._____
3._____
4._____

THE TWO MINUTE MESSAGE

TMM TOPICS BASED ON OUR 'PERSONAL' VALUE (i.e. the value of myself and the other virtual team members)

1._____
2._____
3._____
4._____

6

PULLING IT ALL TOGETHER

THE BUSY PERSON'S SUMMARY TO THE TMM PROCESS

If you have riffled through this book and you've landed on this section by chance, you'll find that it gives you an overview of the two-minute message process. It is intended as a quick reminder / quick reference section. But don't let it stop you reading the rest of the book!

DEFINITION OF A TWO MINUTE MESSAGE
A Two Minute Message (TMM) is a synopsis encompassing the main points of an idea. It is the 'core' of your message or sales story.

There is nothing sacrosanct about the phrase 'two minutes'; your message should be as brief as is necessary to achieve your defined purpose.

A TMM is usually spoken but it can also be a written message. For example as a single page letter in advance of an important telephone call or face to face meeting.

WHEN YOU WOULD USE IT
There are four main purposes for a TMM

- To arouse interest in a topic and to 'earn the right' to further discussion. This is a common sales usage, whereby the caller must justify the time and attention of the recipient. The early stages of your sales call will have this objective so that your targeted client will be genuinely willing (even enthusiastic) to continue the meeting.

- Writing a single page 'promotional letter' has the same objective as the previous example, only it is in written format. The TMM structure is the same as before and the letter is used to pave the way for a meeting, either as a preparatory step to a telephone call or by pre-empting some of the arguments and justifications.

- To put over a 'set piece' story. This too, has the same objective as the first example, but the situation is very often initiated by the customer who might request an opinion, e.g. by saying, ' tell me about ...' There will be topics that your customer will want to discuss and for which you must be prepared.

- As the basis for a larger event or presentation. Your twenty minute (say) client presentation should start life as a TMM synopsis and in a TMM format. This will help you to stay focussed on your objective and to add the level of detail you need to achieve it (and no more). This synopsis will also help you to give a two minute version of your presentation whenever necessary.

THE OATS SEQUENCE
This stands for Objective, Audience, Themes, Synopsis. It is the way I recommend you approach the challenge of building your TMM.

- Be clear about your TMM objective; it will fall into one of the four categories described above, but remember the SMART mnemonic.

    - Make your TMM objective Specific: be clear about the topic about which you want to arouse the client's interest'
    - Make it Measurable: how will you know that the client's interest has been aroused? What affirmation or actions do you seek?

PULLING IT ALL TOGETHER

- Make it Achievable: You must believe that you have a reasonable chance of success (or at least it isn't a ludicrous challenge). Be sure that you are targeting the right person. Can he/she sanction the decision that you seek?
- Make it Relevant: Your TMM objective should fit in with your wider campaign objectives. It will be the first critical milestone that you must reach.
- Make it Trackable: The time-scale from initiation to success is short enough to make this a 'non issue.'

- Identify your target Audience. As far as possible do this in terms of named individuals; not job functions or levels. The more specific you can make this, the better. Remember that a TMM designed for one person may not be appropriate for another. Analyse your audience KAMA (current knowledge & attitudes, the motivation that you want them to have and the actions that you seek). Invariably you will be seeking commitment (and resource). Make sure that your target audience has the authority to agree to your requests.

  Remember that you have 'internal' customers and target audiences as well as the more conventional 'external' ones.

- Identify the main Themes of your message. These are all the points that you need to make in order to achieve your objective. Distinguish between relevant themes and general 'facts' however valid or impressive these might be. Your themes will be your strengths, but remember our definition of a 'strength', i.e. *'something that, if exploited will bring the opportunity closer to realisation.'*

- Construct your Synopsis. This will be your TMM and it should follow the four part structure shown below.

THE FOUR PART STRUCTURE FOR A TMM

- The Audience Context Statement (ACS)
  This will put your proposition or claim of value in the right context. Your ACS should be something that your audience will accept. It will state an accepted customer issue or business statement of fact. It should not say anything about you, your company or your products.

- The Key Theme
  This is your message headline. It should be the single point about what you can offer that will address the substance of your ACS, and which will help you to achieve your objective.

- The Supporting Themes
  This section of your TMM will contain three or four supporting themes (no more). These can either add credence to your key theme (e.g. client references for it), or other different themes that address the issues of your ACS.

- The Closing Statement
  This statement should link back to your objective. It closes the loop of your TMM and requests the commitment that you seek in your objective.

TAKING THINGS FORWARD

You have probably read this book from cover to cover in a single sitting. That's what I intended. Maybe you paused along the way to make some notes or to identify some TMM topics that are relevant to your business situation. That's the first step. If you haven't already done it, reread the book and make your notes as you go along. Write on the pages if you want to.

In the appendix you will see a blank proforma which you can use to create your two minute message. (I suggest you enlarge it to A4 size). I

PULLING IT ALL TOGETHER

am a fan of this document not just because I created it, but because it is simple and there isn't much space in which to write (unless you expand it to A1 size). That will force you to be selective when deciding what to say. Use this document to sort out the substance and flow of your message. You can finalise your precise wording afterwards.

I have also included some TMM examples to show how you would use this document. They are more general than they should be in real life, as I didn't have a specific target audience in mind. You will do a better job with your efforts, I'm sure.

If you get stuck or if you have a question, feel free to contact me. You might want to take advantage of my eTMM service, giving you advice and assistance directly at your time and point of need. Contact me for more information. Or visit the Cambridge Associates website (or click on www.TwoMinuteMessage.com).

Thanks you for your time. I hope your investment of this precious resource helps you to make better use of it in future.

William Freeman
Cambridge Associates
14 Cranmer Road, Hampton Hill, Middlesex, TW12 1DW
Telephone ++44 (0)20 8941 9156
email wdf@cambridge-associates.co.uk
www.cambridge-associates.co.uk

7 APPENDICES

THE TMM PROFORMA

This first part of this appendix contains a blank proforma document and a copy with a brief description of what goes into each of its section.

Use this document to sort out your ideas for a spoken or written TMM, and to put them in sequence. You can enlarge my proforma, or just use the headings in a free-form way, or in some way that suits you. There's no rocket science in this document layout, but most people find it useful.

Get your basic ideas sorted out first before you worry about the precise words or phrasing that you intend to use.

THE TWO MINUTE MESSAGE

BUILDING YOUR TWO MINUTE MESSAGE

TMM Topic	
Target Audience	*TMM Objective*
Audience Context Statement	
Key Theme	
Supporting Themes	
Closing Statement	

BUILDING YOUR TWO MINUTE MESSAGE
EXPLANATION OF PROFORMA

TMM Topic	
This is the working title of your topic. It is for your eyes only, you'll think of fancier words to use with your audience	
Target Audience	*TMM Objective*
The specific individual you want to raise the subject with. Named individual if possible	The outcome that you want from your TMM. What do you want your audience to agree to as a result of it?
Audience Context Statement	
Scene setting statements. Significant business issue or implication that you think your audience would (readily) agree to. Nothing about you or your company here	
Key Theme	
The main point of your message. The single point that you would want your audience to remember. This theme should logically follow from the audience context statement	
Supporting Themes	
a) Evidence (e.g. references) to support your key theme b) Other significant themes that address the audience context statement and help you achieve your objective	
Closing Statement	
A link back to your objective. A statement of what you would like to happen next	

SOME TMM EXAMPLES

The first three examples show the TMM format applied to itself. That sounds somewhat convoluted, so let me explain.

They each take the two minute message process as their topic, but look at it from three different angles. You will see how each TMM example differs, according to the intended audience and the desired objective.

The first of these examples is aimed at book publishers. The purpose of this TMM is to interest them (or at least one of them) in the possibility of publishing a book about this topic. All that I want to do with this TMM is to get a publisher to want to see the idea in more detail. In the terminology of this book, I am buying time to present my case fully. I don't expect my brief letter to get me a publishing contract. Frederick Forsyth might be able to do that, but I cannot.

What I do want, however, is *genuine* interest. This can be difficult to assess, but I know that book publishers are busy people and, in most cases, would not pursue a project unless they thought the idea had merit. You need a bit of trust and faith sometimes (even with book publishers!).

The TMM proforma identifies the key points that I would make (did make, I think). The next step is to take these ideas and draft an appropriate letter, and you'll see my attempt.

There are many ways to skin a cat, of course, so I am not always one hundred percent wedded to <u>exact</u> TMM structure with every letter. But I'm fairly close to it, and any variation is done for a reason.

In this letter I say, up front to these publishers, that I am trying to interest them in a potential book.

They would expect that. They would want that.

BUILDING YOUR TWO MINUTE MESSAGE - EXAMPLE 1
BOOK PROPOSAL

TMM Topic	
The Two Minute Message	
Target Audience	*TMM Objective*
Book publishers	To interest them in the potential of a book on this subject, to the extent that they are keen to view a business case and an outline synopsis

Audience Context Statement

In the competitive business world people constantly need to improve their skills. A new book on a relevant topic has a potential marketplace of many thousands of UK sales people, plus thousands more overseas.

Key Theme

The subject of this book (the TMM technique) shows how people can engage the attention of busy clients (in competition with other demands) and earn the extra time they need to present their case. Most sales skills books (and courses) comment on the importance of this activity. This book (unlike any other) focusses on this critical skill.

Supporting Themes

The book is designed to be around 100 pages, easy to read and with a style and target price that not only fits the business community, but is sufficiently general to be a good 'impulse buy' for a much wider field.

The author's working background and experience give the credibility needed to write such a book. He is also a part-time professional cartoonist and this book would come with accompanying illustrations.

Closing Statement

A detailed synopsis is available for consideration and the first draft would be available for consideration within two weeks.

THE TMM LETTER: BOOK PROPOSAL

Dear Publisher
Proposed Book: The Two Minute Message

I am writing to see if you would be interested in considering publishing this book. It addresses an unexploited niche in the marketplace and is relevant to many thousands of sales people within the UK and abroad.

Sales people are constantly competing for the time and the attention of their clients, and they face fierce competition in doing so. This book describes a technique that will help get the extra time they need to present their case. Unlike any other it focusses on this critical skill.

The book will be around 100 pages, easy to read and with a style and target price that will make it attractive to any businessperson. It will also to be a good 'impulse buy' for a much wider marketplace.

My background and experience gives me the credibility and knowledge to write such a book. I worked many years for IBM as a sales manager and, in my latter years with them, I ran the UK sales training department. In my current role as managing director of Cambridge Associates, I work with other blue-chip organisations helping them to develop their sakes and marketing skills.

If, like me, you are excited by the potential of this book, I would be delighted to send you a synopsis and I could have a sample chapter ready within two weeks. I am keen to move quickly on this project.

Thank you for your time and I look forward to hearing from you. I enclose a stamped addressed envelope for your reply.

Yours sincerely

William Freeman
(keen as mustard and raring to go)

EXAMPLE 2

The second TMM example is also about the two minute message process and it is aimed at people like you, the readers of this book.

It is designed to arouse your interest and curiosity about this topic to the extent that you would want to read the book (or at least flick through it).

I hope you see the importance of the audience context statement. If this doesn't apply to you, or if you think it irrelevant, it is unlikely that you would be attracted to this subject.

If my TMM was successful, you would want to know more about the two minute message process and how you could benefit from it. I hope that it would turn a browser of this book into a buyer of it. So I should put this message where people can see it. Perhaps on the flyleaf.

Even if you have read the book, you might want to know more about the topic or how to develop your skills further - hence my closing statement.

As with the previous example, you will note that the TMM proforma helps to identify the key components of the message. We still need to write the words as they would appear in the letter, book flyleaf or wherever.

If we intend our TMM as part of a face to face or telephone conversation, then we would need to be comfortable about the words and phrasing that we will use, so it becomes part of a natural sounding conversation.

BUILDING YOUR TWO MINUTE MESSAGE - EXAMPLE 2
A TMM DESCRIBING THIS BOOK

TMM Topic	
The two minute message concept (the essence of this book)	
Target Audience	*TMM Objective*
Busy customer-facing people Potential readers of this book	Arouse their interest in the TMM concept so that they would want to find out more

Audience Context Statement

As a business person, you are very busy and so are your clients. You are competing for their time and attention and it is critical to your business success that you can do this

Key Theme

The two minute message process is unique in giving you the ability to crystallise any important 'sales message' into a synopsis that will help you engage the interest of your target audience

Supporting Themes

It is a process that has been tried and proven with a broad cross section of sales people and organisations, each with a variety of sales messages
It is easy to learn and will help you to save personal time in constructing your sales propositions, business cases and formal presentations
The author of the book has worked with numerous 'blue chip' sales organisations and this book distils his knowledge and experiences into an easy to read format

Closing Statement

The process is described in this book with many illustrations and examples. Even when you have read it you are not alone, you can get further information (and on-line assistance) by visiting www.cambridge-associates.co.uk or by telephoning 020 8941-9156

EXAMPLE 3: A SET - PIECE MESSAGE

This third example still has the two minute message technique as its topic. This time I am imagining a situation where someone would ask, "summarise for me how I go about writing a two minute message."

In this example our questioner understands the concept of a TMM but wants an overview on how to write one. In the book we referred to this as a set-piece message.

BUILDING YOUR TWO MINUTE MESSAGE - EXAMPLE 3

A 'SET PIECE' MESSAGE ON HOW TO BUILD A TMM

TMM Topic	
Summary of how to build a two minute message	
Target Audience	*TMM Objective*
Person who asks the question	Summarise the TMM technique so that the questioner is reminded of the key principles (or told them for the first time)
Audience Context Statement	
The underlying principle is based on the fact that you and your clients are busy people. A key part of your job is to compete for, and win, the time and attention of your key customers - internal and external. The TMM process is *the* most effective way to help you do that.	
Key Theme	
The TMM process enables you to build an effective synopsis of our story, so you can: a) gain your customers interest and get agreement to further discussion b) put over a 'set piece' message c) send a promotional letter d) use it as a focus for planning a larger event (e.g. a presentation)	
Supporting Themes	
You start by following the principles of the 'OATS' acronym (define Objective, analyse Audience, identify Themes, create Synopsis) The four point synopsis consists of Audience Context Statement, followed by your key theme, your supporting themes and closing with a statement that links to your objective	
Closing Statement	
Of course, nothing will *guarantee* an effective outcome - but following these simple TMM guidelines will help you to construct the most effective possible message with the minimum impact on your time to do so	

EXAMPLE 4:

THE VALUE OF USING EXTERNAL CONSULTANTS

As you might imagine, this message is fairly dear to my heart. As an independent consultant, people pay for my time and so I must make sure that they get measurable value in return.

Before all of that can take place, however, I need to sell the value of my services, and I must persuade the client that it is worth considering using external consultants to support the activities of his internal resources (or in some cases, replace those activities).

The old chestnut about a consultant being someone 'who borrows our watch to tell you the time (and then doesn't return it)', implies that consultants don't add value, they just do a job of work that clients could do for themselves. For some of my assignments, I would have to put my hands in the air and plead guilty, but I maintain that clients get value from using temporary resources. More importantly, they would too.

Anyway, this next example shows how a consultant offering IT and business skills could try to sell his potential value to an appropriate customer executive. If you are in this line of business, by all means steal any ideas that you think would help you but as you know by now, you will need to tailor your message to a specific audience.

EXAMPLE 4:
THE VALUE OF USING EXTERNAL CONSULTANTS

TMM Topic	
The value of using external consultants	
Target Audience	*TMM Objective*
Customer Executive (e.g. IS Director or HR director)	To raise the topic of using external consultancy resources; to get the customer to consider using them on an imminent project
Audience Context Statement	
The constantly emerging new technologies (internet being the latest example) demand new ways of working to exploit them. You need to do this to maintain your competitive edge. This requires you to have the 'right' combination of skills at the 'right' time'; skills to plan, design, implement and support your new approach.	
Key Theme	
Our external consultancy organisation gives you access to skills and resources as and when you need them. We provide resources to complement your in-house skills on short or long term contracts; whatever suits you best.	
Supporting Themes	
Our partnership network gives us access to a wide variety of resources and skill sets (almost unlimited) Our work with other clients keeps our technology and industry knowledge up to date; we will understand your problem and know how to resolve it	
Closing Statement	
With your current projects, you can plan to use your internal resources in the best possible way, in the knowledge that specialist skills can be made available to you, via our consultancy group. We like to discuss with you how we can add value to your current project.....	

AN OVERVIEW OF CAMBRIDGE ASSOCIATES

We live in a business world of unprecedented change. The speed of Internet development and the deregulation of business boundaries create opportunities to exploit new markets, new geographies and new routes to market. These opportunities also present every business with some major challenges and competitive threats.

We help the senior management of a business to understand this changing environment and to assess the implications on their operations. We help them develop strategies that will exploit opportunities and minimise the impact of challenges and threats.

We offer consultancy, workshop facilitation, mentoring & training programmes and a range of practical sales methodologies that help individuals and organisations to reach their goals.

We run on-site workshops to help our clients apply our TMM process to position their business value. Our on-line eTMM support gives top-level support and guidance when and where it is needed.

See our website for details.

Our clients range from major global corporations to small businesses and start-up operations.

Our popular free e-zine, 'CA Mentor' offers practical hints, insights and tips relevant to all customer facing people. You can peruse the latest issue (and some back-issues) on our website. Better still, why not take out a free subscription?

For more information, visit www.cambridge-associates.co.uk, call us on ++44(0) 20 8941-9156
Or send an email to info@cambridge-associates.co.uk

Straightforward Guides

To find out more about Straightforward Guides, visit our website at:

www.straightforwardco.co.uk
e-mail Info@straightforwardco.co.uk

Alternatively, write to us at: 42 Hollington Road, London E6 3QL. We will forward a catalogue by return.